THE BROKEN POET

TIFF JON

ARPress
ILLUMINATING IDEAS,
EMPOWERING VOICES

ARPress
45 Dan Road Suite 36
Canton MA 02021

Hotline: 1(800) 220-7660
Fax: 1(855) 752-6001

Ordering Information:
Quantity Sales. Special discounts are available on quantity purchases by corporations, associations, and others. For details, contact the publisher at the address above.

Printed in the United States of America.

ISBN-13   Paperback   979-8-89676-013-9
               eBook   979-8-89676-014-6

Library of Congress Control Number: 2024925138

The Meditation Cart

Years ago in the service I had a call in the middle of the night that my children's step mom wanted to take my children away because I did not have money to send home. I was financially strapped but I did pay for all the weekends that my family took them. So in my upset, I saw my roommate had a bottle of bourbon on the kitchen countertop and there wasn't anything to mix it with that but I drank about 2 cups, maybe more, straight. It was about a year since I drank alcohol and it was far more than I needed for being upset. Two days past and I was supposed to go to work and I was dehydrated and dry heaves. A nurse had to come and put my uniform on and take me to the ER but I was supposed to be at work but I ended up with two large bags of IVs and covered my head and eyes with my battledress jacket. I thought the light was going to strike to the back of my brain. Then the doctor said if I knew you were having a party I would have come! And he sent me back to duty and I was wobbling while I walked and I knew it was going to hit the fan for I was weak to work but to my surprise the doctors on my ward put me in the room and told my enlisted I had the flu and two days later I had my elbow resting on the nursing station. And the colonel past by I watched his feet make an about face and he turned and looked at me and smiled. And I was so nervous, my elbow slipped off the nurses station and my head with it cause I was resting it on my elbow and it hit the medication cart still holding up my head. He grinned and laughed and went on his way. Thirty years have past and I think of him and that I still had his approval even though I mess up big time. My mind goes back all the time and me on a medication cart. And when things go wrong for me I think of him and smile.

Heaven

I could see momma laying on her back in a faded blue dress
I said to her "this is not good enough for a funeral"
And then I said "come on momma let go get a cup of coffee"

Time

Time don't go so slowly
Please faster now indeed
For I cannot get this sadness out of my head
Sadness for a reason I don't recall
Felt so hated by all
If I could turn back time
I don't know what to change
For my mind is full of many incidents of misery and pain
My heart is broken right in two
And it can't be fixed by paste or glue
The loneliness is hard to bear
And I cannot understand
For this kind of life was not my plan

Dear God this be me no longer walking
But on bent knee, can you not take away
This insanity
If you find me in all this grief
Melancholy and defeat
It's all around in total despair
Take me Lord in your care

Eden

Adam and Eve in the garden
With all the need
Eve finds the tobacco plant
She rolls it up dry's it and puts flame to it and smokes
And she said "this is good"

And she gives it to Adam
And Adam smokes
And Adam says "this is good"

And God walk through the garden everyday
But they hide and rather not share
What they have found
But God see everything
And he says to them
"I thought it would take you a whole lot more time to learn to smoke
my tobacco plant"

And Eve said "well you were wrong we may be smarter than thee"
God said "I don't know the answer to that really, I only smoke weed"
"But there are no weeds in the garden" Eve replied
And God said, "I know, and it is good"

I'm Shrinking

I went to the psychiatrist today
I talked and talked and talked
And he said to me not one word

I said, "what is wrong with you?"
He said "times up your money is due,
Make an appointment next month and come back."

I said "this is the last you see of me"
He said "if that is true this appointment is free, just bring the other
three"

All Grown Up

When your taught by the golden rule
Children to be seen not listened to
But then you grow up but still so small
For now, you don't talk at all
If you even asked a question, much less debate
Then what do you do
Act like you are two
And you want children round your table
But just caring for yourself
You are not able
And that child that grows up and can speak
Is usually the one called the black sheep
If you consider this to be your plight
It may be a condition that last for life
Many miles away I sit in my room
But still told responsible for someone's gloom
And what do I do but talk no more
To all I shut the door
I'll stay far away
A say to myself till I go blind
For it will always be this or that and on my time
And do I wish I was a child gain
I don't think so I could never win

My Niece

I love my niece so much
Proud to be her aunt, confident and such
But my sister she passed away
She walked into heaven bright day
And how I feel I can't explain
To keep her alive
I tell her all of her mommy's history
I tell her as much as I recall
As much as I can, tell her all
I want her to tell her children everything I say
And hope so much my ow memory doesn't fade
I tell of all our arguments
But realize, she was heaven sent
And I wish for her as much as can be
And make sure she know quite certainly
That I could never replace her mommy
That all day she sites at Jesus feet
And helps place the stars at night
When it is time to sleep

Conflict

If mama told you what to do
But is worked for mama and not for you
And for all your siblings it worked too
So you are felt to be a bad person
And things really worsen
And you go on to be what you chose in life
But can't help but sit back and feel the smite
And think of our whole family so large and big
All from a grandfather from Denmark and did
Not return again
And maybe if I just be more like him
Sprout wings and cross the sea
And them the family that comes from me
Will only have fond memories

The Past

Each day I say I'll start anew
But creeping memories
From my past
They feel brand new
I can't let go, things so old
And with trauma my mind abodes
And what I need or want can't be found
And words "Nevermore" resounds
If I only should
Or only could
Or only would
Change all the things of yester year
Find some clam for this mind
So full of fear
No one wishes to be around me
And person dwelling in tragedy
Shouldn't vent for it's my own misery
I wish I could just comfort
And say I did my best
No that does not happen
And for my mind no rest
In such and abyss it dwells
It is my own personal hell
It has just stopped in it's chosen place
Will I but leave this world a disgrace?
It has just shut the door

It says over and over "no more"
So if I only fathom a better world I left
It a guide, that you do not follow in my footsteps
And even in all honesty
All my cats they too have disappeared
So someone laugh with me
That what I want to hear

Language Barrier

Did I float here on a boat
And from a different sea
Utters words you say don't mean the same to me
Did my even language get so transitional?
When down came the tower of Babel
Yes we understand our language words
But when we say things it is still
Differently heard
Towns, cities, nation all different as can be
But so are lake rivers and seas
And religions and simple petroleum from the earth
Comes out in wars that is the worse
But is that not as bad when things from our youth
That we learn and figure out it's not the truth
Our individual thing, our consciences, and even race
We need to make this world a better place
Competition and our leaders good
And those that should
And that we all give so that in peace we live
There would be no drug pushers
Or people push around
With education and work as we should
And help the ones who only wish they could

And all of us use our talents big and small
Just place it all together and use them all
That the world becomes a better place
And the birth of our children so meek and mild
Will all have their glimpse of Eden as a child

Flower

The center of the flower is the pistil used to reproduce
And the stamen all around it to seduce
And the butterflies and bees you see every hour
As they suckle nectar from the flower
But try not to pick the flower
Let its fragrance be
To sway in the breeze
It requires only stems, roots and leaves
And to pollinate
The legs of bees across it skates

My Garden

On the left side of my sidewalk
I planted vegetables
On the right my flowers
And there were tons and tons of
Leaves on the vegetable side and only few vegetables
And flowers grew big and many blooms

So I drank some coffee and sat the cup on the
Walk beneath me
And I decided next year I will
Plant my vegetable on the right
and my flowers on the left

and I hear a voice say
plant in the middle of the walk
and I pick up my cup that was once
half empty and it was full to the top

and I don't get to plant on either side
for I had moved away

and here all I have is cement
and all I wanted to be a country girl
with dirt between my toes
and what to do heaven knows

Why

Your eyes have died and I know why
But no one asks me why
And I keep seeing your eyes

And in the darkness an eye appears
Is from today or yesteryear
The lid closes
It rolls backwards
And it disappears

And ever so often
One look at me
My frightened mind look
For what to see

And from it's pupil comes this
Silver spray
Like an explosion it vanishes away
And it would not help if I be blind
For the eyes I see are in my mind

And I wish my mind would think
Of beautiful things
Like the blossom of flowers
And gentile rain

And if this frightens you
As much as it does me so
It isn't a poem
It is my woe

And don't try and figure it out
Those of us insane
You figure us out
You be the same

And if only a nightmare
Your mind can concede
Then let me remind you
I'm not asleep

Eyes that look like demons
Do not hurt me so
But the eyes maybe some I know

I've been to east coast
The west, the east China seas
But these eyes I see
Awake or asleep

And with all of life's uncertainty,
I don't want to be you
I want to be me.

Creation

The stars so beautiful tonight
One struck across the sky
And the light it fanned out as
It hit the earth

And like the first creation of God
And from it the earths birth
How miraculous things must be
I wish I was there to see
When he divided the water from the sea
And waves to hit the sand

That was lightness and darkness
All over the sky no source from
Whence it came
Until he created the moon and the
Stars with just His holy name
And out of the dust he created man
And as all of the stars of Abraham

And with his glow
Rainbow in the sky
His promise of protection draws nigh
And a grad rainbow I saw
And for the first time in my life
That hit the earth from one end to the other

In army training
Suppose god gave it to me for in my
Heart many tears were raining
With so much hatred, so much scorn
Try as hard as I could one of my children
Was hurt
Did I join the army to learn to kill
Or I join for I lost all my will
If I could have let go of all the rage
But in the army I wanted to stay

Maybe get enough rank and get them back one day
And I wanted a good job
But I was not able
And all my grandchildren
Don't sit at my table
And I should not have left
My heart be broke
But its just a fine time
For these words to be spoken

Change

I am so lonely all the time
Didn't want it to be that way
Really thought I was quite flamboyant
But must have been more annoy ant

I need to change is what I'm told
And into what I don't know
And I had to get medication
For I could not change
Maybe you just do the same

And if you see me again and I cannot cope
Don't tell me again to change
Or I will have no hope

The white Finch

I had two finch and one was white
They were a gift from my sister
She has so many finches and they had multiplied
I hope to do the same

And one day my aunt came to my house
And said that white finch was once mine
Please give it back to your sister
For I don't want anything to happen to it
And I couldn't keep white finch
And white finch died
She died because my sister let her
Little girl care for the finch
And she thought that the hulls of
The seeds were food
And I felt deep sadness for the finch
I should have kept the one
But I did not want it to be lonely.
Now both are lost

Vacation

I've been in therapy all my life
And still can't get along with even myself
But if you talk to me and I pick up
It's a game
You expect from me the same
If doctor's and nurses I truly converse
And only people like myself is that worse

And I can't comprehend most people at all
And I be the one who should feel so small
Yes I understand all the words you say
But how you said it I don't understand.
That you said it quit that way
And I realize words are as transitional as can be
But try as I will I can't figure out why you said things to me
People to me talk out of their heads
But they want me tied to a bed
They want me in a home
But certainly not their own

Maybe an asylum to get some rest
No one understand what they say or do truly
And I feel like a psychiatrist
On constant duty
And they try to get me in the hospital
And threaten me as they can
But it more a refuge and not a demand

And if I say I'm crazy and unstable
Tell them all they want
Then sending you off to the asylum
The fear more able
Let me digress, we all crazy as the rest
I've done it all I can no longer tolerate
Do it this way, do it that
So if I stop talking, a total wreck
Don't stand there all perplex
Just go on feel total elation
For I have put myself on vacation.

Birthday

When I had my birthday and I was four
My aunt gave me a tea set I adored
I remember being 10 and proudly displayed
All of my fingers on my hands that day
And when I was 13 I was a teenager
But still not aware of life's dangers
A little older I thought I knew everything
Now I wished I knew the same

Life goes on and got really hard
For I learned too late
What I learned too late
What all it did take to make the birthday cake
Birthdays come and birthdays go
And you just hope no one know

And if a birthday everyone miss
And you hear from none
Next year just subtract by one

Birthdays are not like they use to be
Not like they were at one, two or three
And then we wish that in this old world
We did come with each year we grew younger.

Help me Lord

I think about my past
I think through and through
Some terrible thing has happened
Something terrible in my past
If only I knew

I will in my mind
My thinking will not cease
God please give me some peace
Running far away still give no peace of mine
For I carry a darkness with me all the time
I sit and think not a word I say
Will peace of mind every come my way
Year after year no hope in sight
What did I do that was not right
Am I responsible for some terrible deed
Because my heart constantly bleeds
Lord take me far away
Help me have a brighter day
That day never comes
I hope it will
With a mine so cursed, life so tragic
I know I can't deal
From little on and now to old
When things come full circle I recall
What in the world will I say to all

Some brilliant analytical mind
That has shut out the pain
The key threw away
I have run so far from all that can be
And the tragic thing I took me

Unseen Scars

I do feel your sadness
I sorrow for your grief
I do want to comfort you
But I stand here austere
Just a shoulder to lean on
And no words
Please don't question
For I don't cry
I am one of many veterans
With a wound to the heart bud did not die

I want my mommy

Of all the things I think and do
I only think of you
And will I ever see you again
My heart is so uncertain
Where are you my child
Where are you today
Why have you gone so far away
And then I realize with heart so broken
These same words my mother had probably spoken
If I see you again I'll hold you so tight
My arms will grasp you with all their might
But they are empty here tonight
And what stood between me and mama was a feeling
That I would have to travel a sea
To get to her and her to me

Addie Rose

The Addie Rose is tiny as tiny as can be
With tiny blossoms and tiny leaves
On a long long vein to wrap around your heart
Addie was born St. Patty's Day and died 31 hours later

Journey of a Tear drop

I am in in the clouds
And drop to earth
I make puddles and the sea
And don't fear as my particles strike across the sky with so much power
But rather see me in
The mist of a rainbow
And see me in a flower
And when fades and disappears
Look for me in the air

Nothing Impossible

A man that has a dream
Is always rich
And a child that has climbed a tree
Is never poor
And a tree so impossible to climb
He need only to remember in his mind
That he could have held in the palm of his hand
The seed the tree sprouted from

Mermaid Jennifer

Mermaid Jennifer sits by the ocean
Her tail fans out beautifully
And sailors adore her
Know they can never take her home
Her life belongs to the sea

Only Three

How happy life would be
If only at age three
We held tight to our hearts
Tight to our soul
And keep it that way
Till we grow old

Dreams

I don't want to live in dreams
Dreams that don't' come true
If dreams I wish not also for you
So selfishly dreams thinking only myself
And if I but look around
I'd see my dreams in all I have found
So much sadness never to be
If I could only see
That as I look at you
I look at me
And I travel through insanity
Until I realize that love lost
Was always found in me

Military MOS

I liked it in the army
To be all I can be
But the things the finest
I left behind

Years have past by and life goes forward with father time
But I go backwards over and over in my mind
What if I had done that
And why I chose to wear a serviceman's hat
War affects us whether we go or stay
It touches all our lives and in all ways
And war is everywhere and in the country
We fought to be free
Because if I had not been a product of war
And war on drugs and poverty
Till I could no longer be
All I wanted to be: Just mommy.

Author

If it be from sensitivity that an author is born
Then I want to move from my heart to yours
What my fingers too saddened to write
And my breath no words.

Micky Mouse Balloon

You tied my balloon to my hand
I did not like it that way
And I was so small
And would not listen to you at all
I threw this big fit
And on the ground I sit
I want o hold in my hand
And let it so so so high
"Mommy get it back again!"

Best Friend

My Dear friend as we part
It might be a question when
But we may never see each other again
Friendship I always wish would stay
That you could come to me someday

Never I sit and think
Why of me you had a complaint
You no longer do not see
A trusted and loving friend in me
But once you were I accept no less
For you are my friend I called my best
Thought sickness, struggle and sadness pull us apart.
I still keep you close to my heart

I accept in me you have bore your soul
And I will carry you this way
Until we are old
I will cherish it, hang onto it
And pray, till winter blows cold
And I will blame myself
I always do
But think the world of you.

Rain

Rain Harder, rain go away
As Pat and I did play
On our front porch everyday
We thought we could control
The rain if we but only say
Rain harder when softly it rained

And a cool breeze went through on one autumn day
And I knew Pat had gone away
And in the heavens the stars I see
And Pat is saying come play with me.
And the heavens will rain the stars

One Love of a Life

This nightmare I had so bad last night
And you were in my dreams
And my arms around you so fearful for your life
So I called the children to see how you are
And many nightmare come and go and some you for and some you know
And so much sadness I feel in the darkness and still
So most happy to her, you are not ill
It's our anniversary I remember so much
With no reminder, calendar or such
Every year the same
In love with a man I bear his name
And though only together a few short years
I did what I said I would with all my tears
I love you always all these years
And remember when comes again next year.

The Mirror

I am though to be on the wrong side of the mirror
I have taken a good look at myself
And I do not like what I saw
And I truly mean to do better
But I am so crushed that now I am on the other side of the mirror
Trying hard to be loved and understood
And for others to look on the other side
Think the other way and see and hear me
But I am shut out but on both sides now
Just look inside and find me

www.ingramcontent.com/pod-product-compliance
Lightning Source LLC
Chambersburg PA
CBHW031240120626
46545CB00003B/1207